The Adventures of The Stick People

Gary Learns To Love

❧

Christian Pleasant

Zion Pleasant

The Adventures of The Stick People

Gary Learns To Love

Christian Pleasant

Zion Pleasant

The Adventures of the Stick People: *Gary Learns To Love*

Unless otherwise indicated, scripture quotations are taken from the Holy Bible, New International Version.

ISBN-978-098437486-1

Illustrations: Raymond Dockery III

Graphics: Sequester McKinney

Table of Contents

About the stick people

"The Adventures of the Stick People" book series are stories written about a family named the Johnsons that live in Sticktopia, USA. Everything that they encounter usually has a "stick" meaning or connotation. *"The Adventures of the Stick People"* series are based on teaching children how to apply the fruit of the Spirit in their daily lives. Are you ready to learn how to love? Are you ready to learn how to ask others to forgive you when you have done them wrong? Are you ready to learn how to forgive others when they treat you wrong as well? If you are, this book is for you! Enjoy *"The Adventures of the Stick People"* and get ready to learn how to love your friends the way that Gary did!

Dedication

To our daddy, Jamie T. Pleasant who is a perfect example to us of a Godly father. To our mother, Kimberly S. Pleasant, we love you so very much. To our sister, Nikki, you are the best.

To Sequester McKinney, the New Zion Christian Church Family, and to all of our classmates, teachers and administrators at Friendship Christian School.

To Raymond Dockery III, thanks for providing the illustrations in this book. Without you, we wouldn't have been able to complete this project.

Chapter 1

The Big Fight

In the city of Sticktopia, there lives a family named the Johnsons. The father's name is Steve and the mother's name is Lucy. They have two children named Gary and Janet. Janet is 10 years old and Gary is 6 years old. They also have a Grandad that lives with them who is 76 years old. His name is Grandpa Joe. They are a very happy family.

One day as Gary was playing with his friend Kevin, they got into an argument that turned into a fight. After the fight, Gary said, "I hate you Kevin, and I will never be your friend again!" Afterwards, Gary left Kevin and went home.

Gary arrived home and talked to his mom. He told her what happened between him and Kevin. Gary and his mom were getting ready to go to McStickys to eat lunch when Kevin's mom called Gary's mom on the telephone and told her what had happened. Gary's mom was very upset with Gary and asked him, "Why did you tell Kevin that you hate him?" Gary shrugged and didn't give her an answer. His mother said, "Your father will be hearing about this!"

Chapter 2

Gary Must Face His Dad

When Gary's dad came home, Gary was very quiet because he knew his dad was going to discipline him. Sure enough, his dad told him to go in his room, and he would be in there in a moment to talk about what happened. Gary was very nervous because he didn't know what type of punishment he would receive. The longer he waited, the more nervous he became. He was wondering what was taking so long for his dad to come in the room and administer his punishment.

Finally, after waiting a very long time in his room, Gary's dad came in and said, "Gary! I am very disappointed in you son." He continued, "Fighting and telling someone that you hate them is not the way I taught you how to deal with problems you might have with your friends!" Gary replied, "I am grounded aren't I dad?" "No you aren't son." Gary's dad said. Gary was surprised at his father's statement. But he was happy he wasn't going to be grounded.

Chapter 3

Gary's Assignment

Gary's dad said, "I want you to read 1 Corinthians chapter 13 in the Bible and then come to me and tell me what you did wrong." Instead of reading what his father told him to read, Gary snuck out of his room and began talking to Grandpa Joe. Grandpa Joe said, "Aren't you supposed to be reading?" Gary replied, "Uh, not anymore...well, yes I am, but I just don't get it." "Get what?" Grandpa Joe said. "I don't understand the meaning of 1 Corinthians chapter 13 Grandpa Joe?" said Gary. Grandpa Joe asked Gary if his father had forgotten to tell him what the meaning of 1 Corinthians chapter 13 was all about.

After Gary responded that he was never told what it meant, Grandpa Joe said, "Oh! I see now what the problem is." "1 Corinthians chapter 13 is all about love, and what it truly means to love everyone even when you don't agree with each other." Grandpa Joe added, "Gary, what you need to understand about this passage of scripture is that it is the love chapter and shows us how to love others in spite of things they do to us knowingly or unknowingly."

Chapter 4

Things to Think About

Grandpa Joe then told Gary to go back to his room and see if he could figure out how 1 Corinthians chapter 13 related to his fight with Kevin. "Thanks Grandpa Joe," said Gary. "You always give the best advice." "Thanks," said Grandpa Joe. "I have been around a long time and there isn't but one way we should treat everyone and that is with love." He added, "Now go on back in your room and read your scriptures and hurry up because I am cooking tacos tonight for everyone." Gary hurried into his room and started reading 1 Corinthians chapter 13 very intently. After reading 1 Corinthians chapter 13 in the Bible again, Gary came back out of his room and told his mom that he now knew the right way to react to

Kevin and that his behavior was wrong towards his best friend. Gary wanted to tell Grandpa Joe and his dad as well but couldn't find them. He looked in the living room, laundry room, bathroom and basement, but couldn't find them. He then asked his mother where Grandpa Joe and his dad were. His mother replied, "Grandpa Joe and your dad are at the grocery store getting the things they need for the tacos tonight.

"Augh man!", Gary replied. "I was going to tell them that I now know what 1 Corinthians chapter 13 really means." "Why don't you call them on the phone and tell them?" said mom. "Here," said mom. "I will give you my Stickberry cell phone and you can tell them yourself." "Thanks mom, you are the best," said Gary. Gary then called and spoke to his dad and Grandpa Joe and told them that he now knew what 1 Corinthians chapter 13 meant.

Afterwards, his dad told Gary that he should go to see Kevin and ask him to forgive him for his bad behavior. Gary agreed and proceeded to go over to Kevin's house.

Chapter 5

Gary Must Ask For Forgiveness

Gary walked all the way to Kevin's house and rang the doorbell. When Kevin answered the door, he wasn't happy to see Gary. Gary told Kevin hello and Kevin snobbishly said, "What do you want?" Gary proceeded to let Kevin know that he was wrong and asked Kevin if he would forgive him for his bad behavior? Gary said, "Kevin, I want to apologize to you for saying that I hate you." "I really didn't mean that." Kevin responded, "How do I know that you are really sorry for what you said?" Gary replied, "Because I came all the way over here to tell you and ask you to forgive me." "The bible says that we should ask people to forgive us when we do something wrong to them and that is why I am here." Kevin looked at Gary and said, "I not only forgive you but I must ask you to forgive me." "I said some things that were mean to you as well." Gary accepted Kevin's apology as well. Afterwards, Gary told Kevin that he had a new video game, and that they were eating tacos at his house, and he was more than welcome to come over and spend some time with him. Kevin was excited and asked his parents if he could go. Kevin's parents said yes. Kevin and Gary had fun that night and ate all the tacos that their stomachs could hold. They never ever fought again and remain the best of friends to this day.

THE

END

About the Authors

Christian Pleasant is 10 years old and has been a straight A student ever since kindergarten at Friendship Christian School with a 95+ letter grade in all of his individual courses. He is a member of several prestigious gifted organizations including: the Duke Talent Identification Program for gifted youth, Gifted and Talented Program (FCS), The National Society for the Gifted and Talented, Stanford University's Education Program for Gifted Youth, Northwestern University's Center for Talent Development of Gifted Youth and many others.

Zion Pleasant is 8 years old and like his older brother has been a straight A student ever since kindergarten at Friendship Christian School with a 95+ letter grade in all of his individual courses. He is a member of several prestigious gifted organizations like the Gifted and Talented Program (FCS), Stanford University's Education Program for Gifted Youth, Northwestern University's Center for Talent Development of Gifted Youth and many others.

Christian and Zion have both confessed Christ Jesus as their Lord and Savior. They have been water baptized as well. They both play football and basketball and have won championships in each sport.

Epilogue

One of the surest ways to begin to learn how to love the way Gary did is for you to accept Christ Jesus as your Lord and Savior. If you have never done this before, repeat these simple words and you will become saved in Christ Jesus. Repeat the following: Lord Christ Jesus as of this very moment, I accept you as Lord and Savior of my life. I now give my life to you to be fashioned for your purpose and glory. All of these things I have said, I truly believe in my heart and have confessed with my mouth. I know now that I have received everlasting life based on the work that Christ has done at the cross and will continue to do in my life. Lord Christ Jesus, thank you for bringing me to this point of my life where I surrender my all to you. It is in the Holy Spirit through Christ Jesus I say Amen.

Humbly Yours in Christ,

Christian and Zion Pleasant